TRADING STOCK THE PROFITABLE WAY:
The Ultimate Guide on mentorship and managing risk for profitable stock trading.

Caleb Uwak

All rights reserved. No part of this publication may be reproduced, distributed, or transmitted in any form or by any means, including photocopying, recording, or other electronic, or mechanical methods, without the prior written permission of the publisher, except in the case of brief quotations embodied in critical reviews and certain other Noncommercial uses permitted by copyright law.

Copyright © Caleb Uwak, 2024.

Table of content.

[Chapter 1](#)
[Chapter 2](#)
[Chapter 3](#)
[Chapter 4](#)

Chapter 1

Introduction to the stock market.

Companies may raise money on the stock market by offering investors shares of stock, also referred to as "equity." A residual claim on corporate profits in the form of dividends and capital gains is granted to owners of the majority of stocks, along with voting rights.
Additionally, stock markets facilitate the trading of publicly listed firms' existing shares, giving people and institutions the opportunity to invest in businesses in the hopes of making money off of their success or to bet on more speculative short-term price swings. Since the market value of enterprises is determined by the combined activities of buyers and sellers, they are essential to price discovery. Moreover, as public firms are obligated to follow legal requirements and provide shareholders with financial information, stock markets

encourage corporate responsibility and openness.

Stock markets are vital economic indicators that reflect investor mood and provide a gauge of the state of the economy as a whole. Rising stock values often reflect investor optimism about the state of the economy, while declining values might be a warning of unstable economic conditions.

How to Operate the Stock Markets?

Stock markets are structured venues where buyers and sellers exchange publicly traded company shares. These markets are fundamentally driven by the laws of supply and demand, with share values changing in response to changes in the perceived value of firms and general market circumstances. A stock's price usually increases when more people want to purchase it than sell it, but the contrary is also true.

A primary and a secondary market are both facilitated by stock markets. First public offerings (IPOs) of new stocks take place on the main market. Here, businesses raise money for operations or growth by selling investors directly held shares. Once in circulation, these shares go into the secondary market, which is where the majority of daily trading takes place. Investors exchange existing shares among themselves on the secondary market; the corporation is no longer actively engaged in these transactions.

The infrastructure needed to conduct these transactions is provided by stock exchanges, such as the NASDAQ or the New York Stock Exchange (NYSE). They distribute real-time pricing information, maintain orderly markets, and guarantee regulatory compliance. The majority of activity in today's stock markets is done electronically thanks to highly developed computer systems that instantly match buy and sell orders.

The operation of stock markets depends on a variety of market players. Among them are:

Investors who hold shares, both individual and institutional (such as mutual funds and pension funds)
traders with limited time horizons for buying and selling
Market makers, or liquidity providers
brokers who assist with transactions
Regulatory agencies also keep an eye on market activities to safeguard investors and preserve market integrity. When combined, these components form a complex ecosystem that facilitates effective capital allocation as well as investment and wealth generation potential.

How Do Equities Operate?
A corporation that wishes to raise capital splits the entire amount of money it thinks it will require into ownership slices that have a fixed value. These pieces, known as shares, often indicate a portion of a company's ownership. These shares often, but not always, have voting rights and the opportunity to benefit from dividends or

capital gains on the company's earnings. Because they are held by investors rather than the business, the shares that the firm issues to its shareholders are referred to as outstanding shares.

Market capitalization, which varies according to the number of shares issued and the current stock price, is the entire worth of a company's outstanding shares.

The market's assessment of a firm is reflected in its market capitalization, which fluctuates in tandem with share prices.

The Significance of Stock Markets

The stock market is essential to contemporary economies. By letting corporations offer shares to the general public, they provide them access to cash, allowing them to finance development, growth, and innovation. The money that IPOs bring in stimulates economic growth, the creation of jobs, and technical innovation, all of which are good for society as a whole.

Stock markets help allocate resources efficiently in addition to generating cash. They do this via the process of price discovery, in which the combined activities of buyers and sellers decide stock values in real time. This system aids in guaranteeing that funding is allocated to the most auspicious and profitable businesses. Investors convey which businesses they think will prosper and grow—and which ones they may not—by the purchases and sales they make. Overall economic efficiency is promoted by this dynamic process that assists in allocating resources to the most effective applications.

Stock markets provide investors the chance to increase their wealth over time.

Individuals and organizations may invest in firms and share in their financial successes—or disasters. Many individuals may create financial stability and work towards long-term objectives like retirement or paying for school by having access to the stock market. These days, a lot of people depend on stock investments to help them save money for things like retirement, college tuition, and even medical expenses.

Additionally, stock markets are indicators of investor mood and the state of the economy as a whole. Market indexes, like the Dow Jones Industrial Average and the S&P 500, provide glimpses into the overall performance of the market and often represent larger economic trends and expectations. These indicators are widely used by firms, people, and policymakers to guide decision-making in a variety of contexts, including monetary policy, company strategy, and personal financial planning.

The Final Word

The market's beating heart is the stock market, and analysts often use stock prices as a gauge of the state of the economy. However, stock markets are more significant than just places to speculate. They provide businesses with a controlled and organized setting in which they may raise money for operations, development, and innovation, which stimulates economic growth. Additionally, exchanges allow investors to purchase and sell assets, promoting price discovery and liquidity, all of which contribute to the effective allocation of capital.

Furthermore, since listed businesses are obligated to comply with stringent disclosure standards, stock markets foster corporate responsibility and openness. Stock exchanges are important economic indicators that assist analysts and policymakers in assessing the state of the economy by reflecting investor mood and larger economic trends. Essentially, stock exchanges serve as the structural backbone of the financial system, facilitating investor participation and business growth, both of which are critical to the stability and advancement of the economy.

Chapter 2

importance of having mentors in stock trading.

In trading, the significance of mentoring in trading and seeking advice in the markets stands out as a vital ingredient for success. This essay dives into how a mentor may simplify complicated markets, clearly illustrating why a trading mentor is not only advantageous but also required for anybody trying to thrive. We'll coach you through identifying the proper mentor and utilizing their knowledge to solve market issues, develop tactics, and manage risks - crucial parts of sustained trading accomplishment.

Having a trading mentor may fast-track your learning process, minimize errors, and provide you with the emotional support required to hang in adverse situations.

Choosing the proper trading mentor is about finding a good match with your trading style and objectives, plus making sure they've got a great track record and reputation.

Mentorship is like a Swiss Army knife for your trading talents — it puts down a firm strategy, delivers hands-on experience, and helps you conquer your trading emotions.

Imagine walking into an arena where every choice you make might increase your riches or wipe away your money. That's what it feels like to be a beginner in the world of trading. Now, consider having a seasoned coach at your side, someone who has been there, done that, and understands how to navigate the complexity of the market. That's the advantage of having a trade mentor.

Trading mentoring gives individualized coaching to help you comprehend the market, coupled with proven trading tactics and training in autonomous decision-making. This powerful tool may expedite your learning, eliminate mistakes, and deliver the emotional support that's crucial for effective trading.

Why mentoring matters

Trading poses problems comparable to any other career. Despite the temptation of financial freedom and liberty, it implies significant emotional tensions. A trading mentor gives crucial psychological assistance to tackle these obstacles, including coping with market volatility and keeping discipline.
Moreover, a mentor's belief in your potential may improve your own confidence and determination to persist. In summary, having a trading mentor is vital for individualized advice, speeding the learning curve, and gaining emotional support, thereby boosting overall trading performance.

What is mentoring in trading and why is it crucial?

Within the context of trading, mentoring is a relationship where a more seasoned or skilled trader gives instruction to a less experienced or beginner trader. It's a customized guiding system that gives proven trading techniques, educates autonomous decision-making, and offers emotional support. The presence of a mentor may drastically decrease the learning curve, save time, and give obvious avenues for progress.
Thus, mentoring in trading is vital because it speeds learning, minimizes mistakes, and bolsters emotional resilience, leading to greater trading performance.

How can mentoring boost trading abilities and knowledge?

Trading is a skill perfected over time, with mentoring playing a crucial part in its progress. A mentor may provide:
Immediate feedback
Insights that speed the learning curve
Guidance through market complexities
Help in understanding intricate trading patterns and behaviors
They utilize their knowledge to advise traders, helping them become more successful in their trading adventures.
By working with a mentor, traders can:
Receive practical guidance on overcoming challenges and increasing their investment portfolios even after incurring losses
Enhance trading skills and knowledge
Make the process of becoming a successful trader more simplified and efficient.

What attributes constitute an excellent trading mentor?

An effective trading mentor should hold the following qualities:
Relevant skills and expertise in the financial markets of interest to the mentee
A history of strong trading performance over a continuous time
A teaching method that is suitable to the mentee's personality and learning preferences
A desire to give information and skills is needed for a trading mentor. Above all, a genuinely outstanding mentor exhibits a genuine interest in the development and success of the trader seeking mentoring.

Why seek advice in the markets from experienced traders?

Seasoned traders have battled market storms, made and learned from errors, and acquired a lot of information to teach. Their counsel may assist you:

Overcome psychological and emotional biases that might adversely affect trading choices

Gain insights about industry trends

Learn effective risk management approaches to handle market turbulence

In summary, obtaining advice from experienced traders may help you:

Navigate the intricate world of trading

Make informed judgements

Manage risks effectively

Ultimately, became a successful trader.

How can mentoring lessen the trading learning curve?

The route to becoming a great trader may be long and fraught with challenges. However, mentoring may drastically shorten this learning curve. A mentor gives rapid comments and insights, helping traders grasp complicated market dynamics and prevent typical errors. They provide tailored assistance, enabling traders to concentrate on individual requirements and objectives, resolving deficiencies, and strengthening strengths. This concentrated learning strategy speeds the learning process, making it more efficient and effective.

What are the advantages of individual coaching in trading?

Tailored coaching in trading gives a plethora of advantages. It offers specialised coaching, helping traders handle their specific requirements and ambitions. Mentors give emotional support, helping traders control their emotions successfully and keep clear thinking, especially under severe market situations.
They may identify possible chances and hidden possibilities in the market that may not be readily obvious to the untrained eye. Simply stated, individual mentoring delivers a unique combination of practical

instruction, emotional support, and market insights that may dramatically boost trading performance.

How can mentoring assist navigate market volatility?

Market volatility may terrify even the most seasoned traders. But with guidance, traders may learn to traverse these stormy seas with confidence. Mentors with expertise in financial services may give advice on recognizing market patterns, economic data, and the implications of geopolitical events on financial instruments, which is vital during market turbulence.

Moreover, they give insights into effective risk management approaches that assist traders secure their cash and limiting losses. In essence, mentoring can convert the issue of market volatility into an opportunity for development and prosperity.

Why is mentoring helpful for risk management in trading?

Risk management is a fundamental component of trading, with mentoring playing an essential part in it. A mentor may teach traders appropriate risk management tactics to preserve their cash and reduce losses, which is crucial for sustained trading success. A skilled mentor can assist rookie traders in understanding and preventing typical errors, giving insights into the obstacles they will experience and helping them navigate through them more efficiently.

By engaging with a mentor, traders may obtain practical advice on overcoming adversities and enhancing their investment portfolios even after incurring losses. This makes mentoring crucial for learning the discipline of risk control in trading.

How can mentoring contribute to creating a trading strategy?

Formulating a good trading strategy is a vital component of trading, and mentoring may considerably aid in this process. Mentors give proven tactics and insight, assisting traders through market problems and losses. They may assist traders reduce their learning pathways by delivering coaching that helps prevent frequent errors and by sharing key trading ideas. A mentor's approachability, communication skills, and desire to guide are necessary for a productive mentoring experience that helps favorably to build a trader's strategy.

In essence, mentoring may be the spark that converts a rookie trader into a strategic and successful one.

What function does mentoring have in psychological resilience?

Trading requires as much psychological strategy as financial. Market volatility may evoke a broad variety of emotions, from fear and anxiety to joy and greed. Mentorship gives psychological support, allowing traders to develop the emotional resilience they need to endure market volatility, and mentors give constructive comments to keep discipline with trading strategies.

Plus, participating actively with a mentor and confronting real executions may lead to great growth in overcoming psychological trading hurdles.

How does mentoring develop discipline in trading?

Discipline is vital in trading, and mentoring considerably aids in cultivating it. Mentorship in trading improves responsibility by assuring traders:

Keep records of their trades and development, which is vital for assessing performance and finding areas for improvement

Have external accountability that may be more successful than self-accountability

Maintain focus and evaluate trading methods

Having a mentor gives traders with these advantages and helps them remain on course in their trading path.

Daily rituals such as keeping trading notebooks and recording thoughts, feelings, and actions help create discipline and responsibility among traders. In essence, mentoring develops discipline in trading by keeping traders responsible and focused on their trading objectives.

Why is mentoring vital for long-term success in trading?

Mentorship is crucial for sustained success in trading since it fosters:

Adaptability
Critical thinking
Problem-solving
Risk management skills

All of these talents are necessary for sustainable success in a fast-paced workplace. Access to individualized coaching and assistance from a mentor may speed a trader's learning curve and boost their ability to handle complicated market conditions.

The continuous connection with a mentor may give constant assistance, promoting discipline and responsibility in the ever-changing trading environment. Thus, mentoring is a vital aspect of long-term success in trading.

What are the typical hazards of trading without mentorship?

Trading without mentoring might like traveling a strange city without a map. You could finally find your path, but you'll likely take several incorrect turns along the way. Without mentoring, traders may lack the direction to avoid frequent errors that may lead to big losses.

Self-taught traders may have difficulty in building a solid trading procedure and may fall victim to emotional decision-making. Traders without mentors could devote substantial time and wealth to techniques that are unsuccessful or poorly suited to their specific objectives and risk tolerance. The absence of formal learning and responsibility might make it difficult for solitary traders to systematically improve their skills and performance.

Thus, trading without mentoring may lead to a myriad of obstacles, making the route to becoming a good trader a lot tougher.

How can mentoring offer access to useful resources?

In trading, knowledge equals power, and mentoring offers access to a wealth of important tools. These include research tools, trading platforms, and teaching resources that are typically available via mentoring programs. A mentor gives rapid comments and insights, helping traders grasp complicated market dynamics and prevent typical errors. They provide tailored assistance, enabling traders to concentrate on individual requirements and objectives, resolving deficiencies, and strengthening strengths.

By engaging with a mentor, traders may obtain practical advice on overcoming adversities and enhancing their investment portfolios even after incurring losses. This makes mentoring crucial for learning the discipline of risk control in trading.

Why is mentoring especially crucial for beginning traders?

For newcomers, a mentor's help may reveal a clearer route to success by giving a strategic roadmap. While not guaranteed, it may speed up the process of becoming a successful trader. Mentors may teach beginners particular trading abilities and methods that are appropriate to their present level of expertise and money, which is especially advantageous for traders beginning with smaller accounts. A skilled mentor can assist rookie traders in understanding and preventing typical errors, giving insights into the obstacles they will experience and helping them navigate through them more efficiently.

By working with a mentor, new traders can:
Save time that may otherwise be spent on trial-and-error learning techniques that might stretch over years
Save money by avoiding expensive errors
Learn savvy trading tactics

Having a good trading mentor, particularly a day trading mentor, may be highly advantageous for inexperienced traders wanting to locate a trading mentor in the field of forex trading.

What sorts of mentoring models exist in trading?

As there are multiple trading strategies, so too are several types of mentoring in trading. These vary from one-on-one mentoring, where a mentor gives individualized instruction to a single trader, to group mentorship, where a mentor works with a group of traders.
There are also online mentoring programs that give flexibility and convenience, particularly for people who may not have access to a local mentor. Some mentoring programs also provide a blend of these concepts, giving a mix of individual coaching, group learning, and Internet resources.

How does mentoring adapt to individual trading styles?

Just like trading isn't a one-size-fits-all enterprise, the same applies to mentoring. A competent mentor knows that every trader has a distinct style and changes their mentoring strategy to meet that style. For instance, if a trader loves day trading, the mentor would concentrate on methods and approaches that are pertinent to day trading. On the other hand, if a trader likes long-term investments, the mentor will concentrate on methods and procedures that are more suited for long-term investing. This flexibility guarantees that the mentoring is relevant, effective, and valuable for the trader.

Why is mentoring a continual process in trading?

Trading is a fluid industry with continually shifting market circumstances. This demands traders to continuously learn and adapt. Mentorship promotes this process of constant learning by giving updated tactics and insights that help traders remain relevant and successful in the current market circumstances.

The continuous connection with a mentor may give constant assistance, promoting discipline and responsibility in the ever-changing trading environment. Therefore, mentoring is a continual process in trading, helping traders manage the market's ups and downs and steer toward success.

How can mentoring foster a trade network?

Just as a lonely wolf fights to live, a lone merchant may find it tough to prosper. Trading may be a lonely activity, but mentoring can help create a network of traders. A broad mentoring network may supply traders with various viewpoints, ideas, and methods, increasing their abilities and performance in the financial markets.

Mentorship in trading may lead to the establishment of professional partnerships that benefit both mentors and mentees via the sharing of industry-specific skills, knowledge, and contacts. The reciprocal nature of mentoring connections in trading may lead to the creation of a professional network where both mentors and mentees can exchange ideas and opportunities.

What are the ethical concerns in mentoring relationships?

Ethics play a critical part in all interactions, including mentoring. Ethics in mentoring relationships depend on respect, trust, and secrecy. A mentor should respect the mentee's sentiments and rights, keeping a balance in the power dynamic of the relationship. Trust is vital in a mentoring relationship, and a mentor should be dependable and honest, sustaining the mentee's trust.

Confidentiality is another major ethical factor. A mentor should safeguard the privacy of the mentee, respecting their personal and professional limits. By following these ethical concerns, a mentoring relationship may be helpful and fruitful for both sides.

Why is mentoring vital in adjusting to market trends?

The one constant in the trading business is change. Market trends may vary swiftly, and traders need to react to these shifts to be successful. Mentorship plays a significant part in this adaptation process. A mentor may give updated tactics and insights that help traders react to shifting market patterns.

By sharing their expertise and ideas, mentors may benefit rookie traders in the following ways:

Save money that could otherwise be squandered in trial-and-error efforts to follow market trends

Adapt to market trends

Navigate the turbulent world of trading effectively

Therefore, mentoring is vital in adjusting to market trends and navigating the dynamic world of trading effectively.

How can mentoring allow traders to overcome setbacks?

Setbacks are a vital part of the trade process. They might be frustrating, but with the correct direction, traders can learn to overcome them and transform them into chances for progress. Mentorship plays a significant part in this process. By giving strategic assistance and emotional support, mentors may help traders keep their drive and discipline even in the face of disappointments.

Mentorship may strengthen traders in the following ways:

Providing practical advice on handling adversity

Offering assistance in strengthening your portfolios even after incurring losses

Helping traders overcome obstacles and walk the road to trading success.

What function does mentoring play in financial goal setting?

Establishing financial objectives is a critical stage in trading. These objectives give a path to success and help traders keep focused and motivated. Mentorship may play a crucial influence in financial goal setting. Mentors may give advice on defining reasonable and attainable financial objectives depending on the trader's present skills, capital, and market circumstances. They may also give comments and assistance to help traders keep on track toward accomplishing these objectives.

By helping traders create and attain financial objectives, mentoring may play a crucial influence on their trading performance.

Why is mentoring crucial for keeping current on market changes?

Markets are volatile, and staying current on market developments is vital for effective trading. Mentorship may play a vital part in this. Mentors may give insights into developing market patterns and shifts, enabling traders to alter their strategy appropriately. They also give access to tools and industry connections that may assist dealers keep updated about the newest innovations and practices.

By helping traders keep current on market movements, mentoring may play a big influence on their trading performance.

How can mentoring build a feeling of responsibility in trading?

Accountability is an essential component of trading. It requires accepting responsibility for one's trading choices and learning from the repercussions. Mentorship may promote a feeling of responsibility in trading. Mentors help traders preserve records of their transactions and development, which is vital for assessing performance and finding areas for growth.

Having a mentor offers traders with external responsibility, helping to keep focus and verify trading tactics. By developing a feeling of responsibility, mentoring may help traders remain disciplined and focused on their trading objectives.

Chapter 3

Navigating the stock market.

Navigating the Stock Market: 5 Crucial Factors for Buying and Selling Stocks

In the very exciting world of the stock market, knowing the subtleties of buying and selling stocks is crucial for investors. Whether you're a seasoned trader or a rookie investor, here are five key considerations to remember when navigating the convoluted world of stock transactions.

1. Market Research and Analysis: The Foundation of Informed Decisions

Before making any stock purchases, undertake comprehensive research on the firms you're interested in. Examine their financial condition, performance history, and prospects. Research and check financial accounts, yearly reports, and market evaluations to make educated judgments.

Keep an eye on industry changes and economic variables that might impact stock pricing.

2. Risk Tolerance and Investment Goals: Tailoring Strategies to Your Profile

Define your risk tolerance and investing objectives explicitly. Different equities come with varied amounts of risk, and recognizing how much risk you're ready to face is key. Whether you're striving for long-term growth or short-term rewards, connect your stock transactions with your financial goals.

3. Diversification: Spreading Risks for Stability

Diversification is a crucial factor in controlling investment risk. Instead of placing all your assets into one stock, distribute your investments across multiple sectors and businesses. This method helps lessen the effect of poor-performing equities on your total portfolio and offers a more steady investing plan.

4. Stay Informed on Market Trends: The Power of Timely Information

The stock market is impacted by a number of variables, and being educated is your greatest protection against unexpected market fluctuations. Regularly follow financial news, corporate announcements, and market movements. Embrace technology tools that deliver real-time data and insights, helping you to make timely and educated choices.

5. Transaction Costs and Fees: Understanding the Financial Implications

Every stock transaction comes with accompanying charges, including brokerage fees and taxes. Be mindful of these fees and include them in your investing selections. Choosing a trustworthy brokerage with clear cost structures may greatly affect your total profits. Consider the long-term effects of transaction expenses on your investing plan.

Conclusion

Buying and selling stocks in the market is both an art and a science. Remember, the stock market is dynamic, and your investing plan should develop appropriately. Continuously educate yourself, adjust to market developments, and consider obtaining guidance from financial specialists to maximize your stock trading experience. With a well-informed strategy, you may harness the potential of the stock market for long-term financial success.

Chapter 4

Managing risk for profitability.

Top 7 Risk Management Techniques for Successful Trading.

Risk management is a fundamental part of trading and investing, allowing traders to preserve their cash while maximizing possible earnings. Whether you are a day trader, swing trader, or scalper, utilizing proper risk management tactics is vital for attaining long-term success in the financial markets. In this post, we will cover the top 7 risk management tactics that may assist traders traverse the markets with confidence and discipline.

1-Have a Trading Plan:
A well-designed trading strategy functions as a roadmap, offering clear instructions and procedures to follow before making any deals. It demands traders to completely comprehend their strategy and aims, therefore avoiding spontaneous choices and emotions-driven behaviors. A trading strategy should contain defined trading

objectives, techniques for entering and exiting trades, risk tolerance levels, suitable position size criteria, and stop-loss levels to minimize possible losses.

2-The Risk/Reward Ratio: The risk/reward ratio is a key concept in risk management that analyzes the prospective profits against the potential losses in a transaction. By calculating this ratio before making a transaction, traders may decide whether the risk is worth incurring depending on their trading approach. A greater risk/reward ratio enables traders to remain successful even with a lower win rate, underlining the significance of establishing a balance between risk, profit potential, and tolerable losses.

3-Stop Loss/Take Profit Orders: Implementing stop loss and take profit orders is vital in preserving your money and achieving gains. A stop-loss order automatically terminates a trade when the market hits a preset price, reducing possible losses. On the other side, a take-profit order locks in gains by closing a trade when a predefined profit objective is met. It is vital to stick to these orders and avoid straying from the trading strategy, since hasty modifications may lead to unneeded losses.

4-Selection of Assets and Time Intervals: Choosing the correct assets and time intervals that match your trading style, objectives, and risk management plan. Factors to consider include accessibility, liquidity, volatility, correlation, and your experience. Each asset class contains distinct characteristics, and picking the ideal time periods is critical for capturing your desired market movements. Shorter time intervals are good for regular traders, while longer intervals suit investors and swing traders.

5-Backtesting: Backtesting includes testing trading techniques using past market data to assess their efficacy. By replicating historical trading situations, traders may acquire insights into their strategies' success, discover strengths and shortcomings, and adjust their techniques appropriately. While backtesting is a vital tool for risk management, it is crucial to understand that previous success does not guarantee future outcomes.

6-Margin Allocation: Managing margin allocation is crucial to minimize overexposure to any one deal. Traders should avoid dedicating a major percentage of their cash to a single deal since unanticipated market developments might lead to huge losses. Adhering to basic standards, such as limiting the allocation percentage to 1% of every transaction, helps protect the entire portfolio from large drawdowns.

7-Diversification and Hedging: Diversifying your portfolio and adopting hedging measures decreases risk exposure and offers a safety net against unexpected market fluctuations. Diversification entails investing in a variety of assets across several industries and asset classes, limiting dependence on any one holding. Hedging includes employing assets that adversely correlate with other holdings, giving a buffer during market downturns.

Conclusion: Effective risk management is the backbone of effective trading and investment. By having a well-defined trading strategy, knowing the risk/reward ratio, executing stop loss/take profit orders, and considering asset selection and time intervals, traders may reduce losses and safeguard their cash. Backtesting helps traders to fine-tune their strategies based on previous performance, while appropriate margin allocation, diversification, and hedging assist secure their portfolios. Embracing these risk management approaches helps traders traverse the markets with confidence and discipline, enhancing their prospects of long-term success.

www.ingramcontent.com/pod-product-compliance
Lightning Source LLC
Chambersburg PA
CBHW070948220526
45471CB00007B/2946